Dear Me.

Andrew Yang

To learn more about my journey:

iamandrewyang.com
instagram.com/iamandrewyang

Book Cover: Andrew Yang

This book is dedicated to all the incredibly courageous women in my life who have positively influenced, inspired, and motivated me over 30 years to become who I am today.

Grace, Michelene, Leanne, Lorena, Megi, Gresa, Teuta, Rina, and most importantly...

Hee-Kyoon Kim. My beloved Grandmother.

Thank you all.

Contents

Dear Me.

Better Than Yesterday.

Dear Me.

This year has been one of the hardest years of your life.

You've won and you've lost.

What is it all for.

A striking yet elegant question you need to be asking yourself.

There is no right or wrong answer.
Tis is much of life.

You can overcome this.
You know you can.

You know who you are.
Don't fucking lose it.
Keep it together.

Find the love within yourself that's elevated you to where you are today.

This will be one of the hardest journeys you will take and you need to take it alone.

Be better than you were yesterday.

Whatever that means to you.

Love.
- Yourself

3 Types of People.

Dear Me.

There are 3 types of people in this world.

Those that will hold you back.
Those that will hold you now.
Those that will hold you into the future.

It's your fucking choice who to call your *"friends."*

I choose the latter.

Either we grow and suffer together or you suffer on your own.

Love.
- Yourself

One Day.

Dear Me.

You've learned to be happy alone because you never want to hurt anyone.
You've learned to check your ego so you can learn from everyone.
You've learned to let go because you can't bear to see anyone else get hurt.
You've learned that there are very few things in this world that warrant your deep emotions.

But it still hurts.

Knowing that one day.

It will all happen again.

Love.
- Yourself

New Chapter.

Dear Me.

Do you feel it.

Your old life fading.
But a new one beginning.

Things are changing.
This is your next step.

Whatever happened. Happened.
Whatever will happen. Let it happen.

Be grateful for what life put you through.

You are now stronger and better than you were.

To new chapters.
To all the times you will fuck up.
To all the times you will be a good person.
To new adventures.

To the world.

Love.
- Yourself

Deep Soul.

Dear Me.

You must learn that a deep soul means learning to accept that we live our lives incomplete.

As hard as it is we must let go of the hurt of the past.

But even more painful is learning to let go of the present and sometimes even the ideal dreams we place in our minds of the future.

You must be in a constant state of growth.

The universe doesn't define you.
The universe defines itself.

No one will truly understand you and push for your future except you.

We're all fighting for something that is deeper and darker than any words can explain.

So keep going and never stop.
Don't hide.
Face yourself and you alone.

Love.
- Yourself

It's Time.

Dear Me.

It's time.

Never forget this feeling.

You are better than yesterday.

The last 2 weeks have been the most life changing moments of the last 3 decades.

We live in a world of billions interconnected by six degrees of separation at the push of a button.

But it takes tremendous strength and power to trust and to focus today.

With great power comes great responsibility.

Keep your friends close and your enemies closer.

It's never truly over until someone gives up.

Do you want it to end?

Love.
- Yourself

Live.

Dear Me.

Don't get too caught up at a single point in life.

Life is but a grand story that makes you who you are.
That is told through the ages.

That will evoke a raw emotion to all those who listen.
You choose that emotion.

Your grand story is yours and yours alone.

You can't choose how it begins.
But you can choose how it unfolds.
And how it ends.

Live. Love. Laugh.

But more importantly.

Share. Listen. Learn.

Love.
- Yourself

Until The End Of Time.

Dear Me.

Your grandmother raised you to be no fool.
Your grandmother raised you to not fuck around.
Your grandmother raised you to be Powerful. Independent. Loyal.
Your grandmother raised you to be the best human being you can be.

Do not take her life lessons for granted.

She's taught you more about yourself and about humanity than any other person on this planet.

She's taught you the value of women. That we are all human.

We all deserve the same Rights.
Opportunities.
And Care.

She's been through more in her lifetime than you can even fathom in today's era.

She's taught you that every obstacle, no matter how big, can be overcome.

Every. Single. Fucking. Obstacle. Can. Be. Overcome.

She's taught you to take a bullet for those you truly care about.
She's taught you to let go of those that think any less of you.
She's your rock and forever will be.

She's tattooed on your arm.
But she's also tattooed in your heart.

Until the end of time.

Love.
- Yourself

Never.

Dear Me.

Never be like your father.

Never run away from your responsibilities.
Never run away from your problems.
Never live a life of delusion.

You can choose your friends.
But you can't choose your family.

And unfortunately you got fucked by this.

You are accountable to your own actions.
You have no one. no place. nothing to blame except for yourself.
You live your life the way you want to live it.

If you fuck up. It's your problem. Solve it.
If you lose balance. It's your responsibility. Find it.
If you achieve. It's your success. Live it.

Your father was never there for you during the best times.
Your father was never there for you during the worst times.

Sadly that was for the best.
Be grateful he wasn't.
Let go.

You already said goodbye.

Actions speak louder than words behind all the excuses and lies.
Never say shit you don't mean.
Prove it. Live it.

Be the better human being.

Be the human that your father wishes he could have been to you.

Love.
- Yourself

3 Decades.

Dear Me.

You thought you had it all figured out when you turned 30.

You thought 3 decades of chaotic and fruitful moments were behind you.

You thought you were the best version of yourself.

But you were wrong.

Age is truly nothing but a number.
Experience is undefined and priceless.

It's time to expand beyond your horizons.
Beyond yourself.
Beyond this land.

There is no perfect utopia.

But you can and you may bring utopia to yourself.

There is much to explore.
Life is but a beautiful legacy.
Life can also be a complete bitch.

Onwards to the next destination my dear friend.

To the lives of the brave.
To the lives of the complacent.
To the lives of those who dare to seek more.

Love.
- Yourself

Canada.

Dear Me.

You now know why she chose Canada.
Why she spent days on a boat just to get here.

It wasn't to get away from war.
It wasn't to run away.
It was to provide.

In the most selfless act of human nature.
It was to give her future a chance at freedom.
A chance at living in a world of opportunity.

As diverse. As innovative. As supportive we are as a nation.
We are also lonely. concrete. individualized.

But she still chose this nation despite all that.
Anything was better than turmoil and destruction.

We say we are the True North. Strong. And Free.
Among the world. We are.

It takes extreme discipline and focus to make it in this nation.
It takes years of blood, sweat, and tears to leave a mark.
To leave a contribution that you are a part of this nation.

Through it all.
Just to be called a citizen.
Just to receive that pocket travelling book.

To be welcomed into every part of the world with open arms.
To be welcomed into every part of the world meaning no harm.

Despite high taxes contributing to the system.
Putting all our trust into a system that supports us as humans.

To have access to innovative and free healthcare.
To have access to a rich history of worldly relationships.
To have access to a true supportive system.

That is the beauty of her mind.
That is what she wanted for the next generation.

She suffered to set you free.
Not in a single country.
Among the world.

You owe her your life.
Thank her. Support her.
Do it all in the name of her.

Thank you Grandma.

Love.
- Yourself

Mediocrity.

Dear Me.

Refuse to live a life of mediocrity.
Refuse to be controlled by the lost souls around you.
Refuse to survive.

Choose to thrive.

You are better than every yesterday that stood by you.
You have learned to live a higher standard.
You have learned to thrive where few can breathe.

And this wasn't accomplished by following the ways of life of
everyone else.

This was accomplished by surrounding yourself with the right people
that push you forward.
This was accomplished by choosing to be different than everyone
else.
This was accomplished by shutting the fuck up. Listening. And
learning. Then choosing your own path.

Ya you fucked up along the way because you didn't listen with
enough intent.

But if life were a perfect utopia.

We'd all be living our best lives.

But alas. We're not.

You choose to live your life everyday aiming for the stars.
Aiming for your future.
Aiming to live a life that you want to live every single day.

Do it and don't fucking lose it.

Love.
- Yourself

Ego.

Dear Me.

Don't be a fucking idiot.
Check your ego at the door.

If you think you know everything then what is there to live for.
What is there to learn.
What is there to wake up to every morning.

It was the great Albert Einstein that once said.

"The greater the knowledge. The lesser the ego.
The lesser the knowledge. The greater the ego."

No one got anywhere in life thinking they had it all figured out.

Life is a journey filled with timeless offerings of knowledge and
memories that shape each and every individual in their own unique
fashion.

Accept yourself for where you are.
Accept yourself for you are always learning.
Accept the truth on whatever basis you believe that to be.

You believe in the fundamental truths of science.
As inexplainable as some things are that you have witnessed and
experienced.
If that is your truth than accept that you don't know it all.

We live in an ever-expanding cosmos.
There is always something new to discover.

You are always seeking knowledge until the day you lay to rest.

Love.
- Yourself

Everything Happens For A Reason.

Dear Me.

Is it real.

That everything happens for a reason.
That you must learn to love yourself.

Yes. Yes it is. But.

As with many things in life.
There are levels.
There are depths.

You went through life thinking things were black and white.

That got you far. No doubt.

It's time to think deeper.

Because there are depths to you that you can't even fathom.
You haven't even realized yet.

Go. Go deep.

It will take a lifetime.

You are always learning new things about you that you may love.

And you may also hate.

Let go of what you hate.
And continue to love.

Everything that has happened. Happened.
To make you the person you are today.
That is your reason.

It's made you realize you did what you did out of love and respect for
yourself.

And knowing the dangers of you when you're alone.
You did it for others.
In a selfless act.

Keep moving.
There's more to discover.

Love.
- Yourself

Where You Need To Be.

Dear Me.

Why do you care so much.
Why do you care what people think.
Who the fuck cares if they judge.

That's their problem.
Not yours.

You never cared before.

Why are you caring now.

Stop wasting your time.

You are exactly where you need to be.
That's enough.

Now go be you. The authentic and true you.
The you that you have always been.

There is nothing wrong with that.

Those that see your potential will support you.
Thank them always.

Those that don't will judge you.
Don't let them bring you down.

Take over the world.
Inspire.
Live free.

Love.
- Yourself

Wake The Fuck Up.

Dear Me.

Hey you fuck.
That's enough.
Wake the fuck up.

Stop wasting your time.
Are you seriously just going to let the minutes slip away.

Every step. Take it with purpose.
That you are going somewhere.
And it's exactly.
Where you know.
You need to be.

Channel this emotion.
Use it.
To create your life into something beautiful.

Get some sleep.
And wake the fuck up ready to seize the day.
And all it has to offer.

This is it.
Don't you let it fucking slip.

Love.
- Yourself

Wrong Way.

Dear Me.

ARE YOU DONE.
WHAT ARE YOU DOING.
YOU'RE GOING THE WRONG FUCKING WAY.

DREAM.
DREAM OF YOUR FUTURE.

DON'T YOU FUCKING GIVE UP NOW DIRTBAG.

CHASE IT.
WANT IT SO BADLY THAT YOU WON'T COMPROMISE FOR
ANYTHING.

IT'S YOURS.
LIVE IT.

Love.
- Yourself

Higher Standard.

Dear Me.

You hold yourself to a higher standard.
You are better than this.

Do not let anything take that away from you.

Period.

Love.
- Yourself

Cut.

Dear Me.

Yo. Okay.

Let me talk to you mano a mano.

This is real talk.

You live in a city where everyone is trying to make it.
There's only a small segment of the population that is actually living
their true lives.

You fucking know this.

This is why you had to cut out thousands of people from your life.

So you don't get taken advantage.
So you don't hate everyone.
So you don't lose your fucking mind.

You cut them off because they talk the talk.
But have failed to prove that they walk the walk.

Everyone can talk big.
But actions speak louder than words.

Do not be one of those people.
No.
Not like everyone else.

"If they are not there for your failures.
Don't expect them to be there for your successes."

So knock it off.
Cut them off.

Love.
- Yourself

Paradoxical Selfishness.

Dear Me.

Is there any solace in being selfish.

When you stop thinking of everything around you.
When you only focus on your health.
Your wealth.
Your love.
Your happiness.

Yes.

When you focus on yourself.
You let nothing get in your way.
You destroy all obstacles.
You become a better version of you every day.

No.

You lose touch with reality.
You lose the ability to love.
You lose the ability to appreciate.
You lose chances.

As with all things in life.
There is balance.
Too much of a good thing can mean your self-destruction.

You've lost it all once before.
You were too selfish.
You lost balance.

What you gained was knowledge of your own hell.
The hell that you never want to go back to.
The hell that you vowed you never want anyone else to feel.
Now step forward.

Present yourself to your hell.
Hold your head up high.
For you've moved onto a life.
Far better than your darkness.

Love.
- Yourself

Love.

Dear Me.

Love.

A word of elegance.
A word of beauty.
A word of sorrow.

A word with an infinitely deep meaning.
A word that encompasses an infinite number of unique emotions.
A word that brings you pure joy and utter sadness.

Creativity is spurred by emotion.
The creation and portrayal of emotions in reality.

It's all around us.

Music. Movement. Colors.
Diversity. Health. Architecture.

Do not put it aside.

As hard as it is.

It's what has fueled you.

Every past love has made you a better person.
They have motivated you.
They have inspired you.

You have to thank them for their absence.
For letting you go.
For allowing themselves to love themselves.
Just as much as you do yourself.

Keep telling yourself.
"To hell if I'm going to be left behind."

I've told you once. I will tell you again.
Be better than yesterday.

Love.
— Yourself

Be The Limit.

Dear Me.

Alright bud!
Let's do this!

Let's fucking goooooooooooooooo!

Bust your ass.
Stay disciplined.

Time to level up.

Put in the fucking work.
Wake up every morning ready to fucking kill it.

Remember your dream.

Let it fuel you.

Remember to take breaks for yourself sometimes.
Because you fucking deserved it.

Remember to celebrate those special small successes.
Because you fucking deserved it.

But every other time.

You're gonna chase that dream.

Push yourself to the limit.
Experience your own limit.
Be the limit.

Take over the world.
Don't take what you have for granted.
Share it with the world.

Let's fucking do this.

I'm always here for you.

Love.
-Yourself

Discipline.

Dear Me.

Focus.
Do not get distracted.

Something you tell others but at times fail to tell yourself.

Welcome to the world.

In a time when you can achieve anything you want.

Anything you want.
Behind closed doors.
Only opened by the unique pattern.
In your fingertips.
Or the unique beauty of your face.

With more resources.
With more opportunity.
With more passion.

But with all these resources.
These opportunities.
These passionate people.
Means more distractions.

More chances to consume.
More chances to experience.
More chances to distract you from your future.

It's a blessing and a curse.
You have to earn it.
You have to pay to play.
You have to sacrifice.

You once said.
"It takes more discipline now than ever before to create more and consume less."

Practice what you preach.

It got you this far.

Do you want to be a liar.

I fucking thought so.

Love.
-Yourself

Comfort Is In Your Future.

Dear Me.

Yes.
It's fucking cold.
Winter is coming.

You want to be warm.
You want to be comfortable.
You want to hibernate.

So you're just going to let mother nature control your life.
So you're going to pause everything for her.
So you're going to let her bring you down again.

No.
You won't have any of it.

This is Darwinism.
Only the strongest survive.

Don't turn on the heater.
Don't go back to bed.
Wake the fuck up and raise your internal.

Get your ass moving.

Go to the gym.
Go dance in your underwear.
Go for a walk.
Stretch.

Push beyond comfort.

Movement is beautiful.
Movement is energizing.
Movement is warmth.

Your comfort is in your future.
Not now.
You still got a lot to do.

Your survival depends on you.
And you alone.

Love.
-Yourself

Rock Bottom.

Dear Me.

Remember the days when you almost lost it all.
When you lost balance.
When you feared waking up every morning.
Feared facing your own reality.

It's a dark place.

A place of lost souls.
A place of lost motivation.
A place that locks you into your cruel life.

In an endless paradox of despair and desperation.

Do you want to go back to that.
Do you want to be dependent.
Do you want to face that regret.
Again.

No.

So go.
Far beyond those days.

You vowed to yourself.
To never go back to that hell.

So don't.

Do everything.
Push yourself.

To never feel that darkness again.

Some say.
"The foundations of your life begin after you've hit rock bottom."

Go.

Love.
-Yourself

Fuck You.

Dear Me.

"Fuck you."

The words behind your growth.

To every person who questioned your potential.
To every person who doubted your worth.
To every person who said it couldn't be done.

"Fuck you."

To every person who bullied you.
Threw you into trashcans.
Shoved you in rosebushes.
Punched you in the face in front of the whole school.

To every person who hurt you.
Who made you cry.
Who made you feel worthless.
Who made you question your own values.

"Fuck you."

To every person who left you for dead.
Who took advantage of you.
Who manipulated you.
Who talked shit about you.

"Thank you."

The words you usher to the same people.
For making you who you are today.

Love.
- Yourself

Setbacks.

Dear Me.

Stop getting caught up in every setback.

They fucking suck.
I get it.

But they happen for a reason.

No one ever said life was easy.

Look at the people around you who are living their best lives.

Some know it.
Some don't.

But they all built their self-motivation from setbacks.

It's like a rope is tied to your hip.

Pulling you in.
Pulling you into comfort.
Pulling you into complacency.

But the more you resist.
The more you push forward.

Passed every obstacle.
Passed every wall.
Passed every setback.

The happier you will be.

That's why you told yourself.
Celebrate the small successes.

Because those are the moments.
The moments when you feel it.
You feel alive.

You come up for air.
To start a new adventure.
An adventure.
Better than the last.

With new goals.
New horizons.

That can.
That will.
Be you.

Love.
- Yourself

Everyone Learns Differently.

Dear Me.

Aren't you fucking fed up.
With people.
With lost souls.
Telling you what to do.

Like you haven't experienced it all before.

Clearly some people don't listen.
With enough intent.
An intent to learn.

Learn from your fuckups.
Learn from your traumas.
Learn from your suffering.

It's a paradox.
To get to this point.

You did the exact same thing.
You didn't listen.
You didn't accept how you learn.
You didn't know better.

So you fucked up.
Royally.
But you learned.

Everyone learns differently.

You learn by doing. Kinesthetic.
Some learn by seeing. Visual.
Some learn by hearing. Audible.
Some learn by absorbing. Reading and writing.

You know more about yourself now.
About how you learn.

It's taught you to shut the fuck up.
Live in secrecy.
To never tell anyone about your grand plans.
Your grand future.
To show them instead.

Because.
My dear friend.
No one needs to know.

Except you.

That's you.
That's how you learn.

Love.
- Yourself

Be Proud.

Dear Me.

Be proud.

Proud of who you are.
Proud of your honesty.
Proud of your openness.

Proud that you have failed.
Proud that you have lost.
Proud that you have weaknesses.

That is you.

You have knowledge.
You have strength.
You have a unique identity.

You crave what others fear.
You hunger for independence.
You prey on experience.

Be human.
Be authentic.
Be you.

Love.
- Yourself

Her. She. Family.

Dear Me.

Leave her name in legacy.
Let the world chant her name.
Let the world know who she is.

She is the strongest woman you will ever know.
And the world deserves to know her name.
And be inspired by her story.

That she stood by her children.
That she stood by you.
That she stood by herself.

For family.

Love.
- Yourself

A Child.

Dear Me.

You've told yourself this ever since you were a little child.

During those dark days.
When you hated yourself.
For what life has given you.

Those days.
When you asked yourself why.

Those days.
When you felt.
Felt it was easier to give up.

You learned.

There are two paths you can choose.
Every time you hit a wall in life.

You can choose.
To give up.
Or conquer.

One will end all the pain.
One will make the pain worse.
Before it gets better.

But it does get better.

After forcing yourself to face your pain.
Face your storm.
Face your fears.

Beyond the storm is light.

You will never forget that day.

For it's made you a better human.

A child.
Curled up in the darkness of his room.
Ready to give into death.
But instead chose to take on life.

That is you.
You chose the right path my dear friend.
And I am happy you did.

Love.
- Yourself

It's All You.

Dear Me.

You're tired of drinking socially.
You're tired of the same old conversations.
You're tired of monotony.

You want more.

You want to drink to success.
You want deep conversations.
You want diversity.

You want more.

You want to push yourself to new heights.
You want others to finally pursue their dreams.
You want to live a life of meaning.

You want more.

You want that feeling of achieving something for yourself.
You want that feeling of supporting someone to reach theirs.
You want fulfillment as a human being.
A social creature.

You want future.
You want purpose.
You want freedom.

Make it a need.
A necessity.

Then it will become your self-demand.

And once you achieve it.
It will become your new standard.

With its own set of adventures.
Moments.
People.

People who can.
People who will.
Keep up.

It's all you.

Love.
- Yourself

You Never See.

Dear Me.

What if I told you.

That the happiest people in the world.
Are the ones you never see.

You won't see them on TV.
You won't see them posting selfies.
You won't see them on Instagram.

Because they can do what they want.
When they want.

They don't have to capture every moment.
They live it.

Every single day.

Because they are free.

Free in health.
Eat well. Stay active.

Free in wealth.
Be smart. Save. Invest.

Free in love.
Have it or don't. Love life.

Free in happiness.
Found deep within.

They made sacrifices.
They made priorities.
They made decisions.

They took control of their lives.

That's what you want.

Dream it.
Chase it.
Get it.
Live it.

For it is possible.

Love.
- Yourself

For That Feeling.

Dear Me.

You feel it now.

You've built yourself up so much.
For 30 years.

To become who you are today.

But take a step back.
Just one tiny step.

And realize that you did lose touch of reality.

You're surrounded by artificial.
Fakes.
Materials.

And you lost a sense of yourself.
As a human.

A human.
By nature.

Needs a sense of belonging.
Needs a sense of loyalty.
Needs a sense of comfort.

Through knowledge.
Through trauma.
Through minds.
Through hearts.

A sense of family.

We can only survive alone for so long.
Before nature gives you what you deserve.

Be fortunate.
That it took this long.
To find that feeling.

Relish in it.

For that feeling.

Is happiness.

Love.
- Yourself

I Can't Help You.

Dear Me.

Fuck. Why do you keep going back.

What is it about the past that is bothering you.
What is it that you want to hold on to.
What is it that you found so special.

That is worth that much of your mind and heart.

The compassionate side of you wants to reminisce.
Wants to hold on to a future.

The competitive side of you wants to let go.
Wants to prove yourself beyond the hate.

But you are conflicted.

Do you want to show what you can do.
Or do you want to escape.
Run.
Run away from it all.

Because it's easier.

Or is it your impatience.
Are you looking for the fastest answer.

Something that will mask the pain.
Something that will make you feel good now.

But will never solve the true problem.
The source.

It's your decision.
I can't help you here.
I wish I could.
But I can't.

Will you face the pain.
Or run from it.

Eventually you will always have to face the truth.
No matter how long you try to run from it.
No matter how hard you try to avoid it.

Are you delaying the inevitable.

Love.
- Yourself

It Is Easier.

Dear Me.

I get it.
And it's the harsh truth.

It is easier.

It is easier to give up.
To leave it all behind.
Like nothing ever happened.

And we are.
Individually.
Just a tiny.
Minuscule.
Piece of the entire puzzle.

The puzzle of infinite pieces.

For which we call.
Our reality.
Our space.
Our time.
Our moment.

You can choose to give up and live as you are.
For the rest of your short life.

Or can you take everything in.

Every sight.
Every experience.
Every moment.

That makes this reality worth it.

And make the change.
With every step.
You make sacrifice.
But you do not let that sacrifice go in vain.

You live with no regrets of every moment that happened until now.
This moment.

You know you can do it.
And it will take years.
Fuck. It may take your entire life.

But if you can lay on your death bed.
With a big ass fucking smile.
That you did everything you could have possibly done.

Then that my dear friend.

Is a life well lived.

Love.
- Yourself

Trust.

Dear Me.

I guess it is true.

You really can't trust anyone except yourself.

Fuck.

That trust.
Honesty.
And loyalty.
Are truly that hard to find.

But we live in a world of billions.
Across 197 countries.
Across 7000 cultures and languages.

And every single human is unique.

You just gotta keep learning.
You just gotta keep moving.
You just gotta keep trying.

Sometimes.

That's all that matters.

Love.
- Yourself

Simpler Life.

Dear Me.

Sometimes I do.

Sometimes I do miss the simpler life.

When we didn't have so much to consider.
So much to take in.
So much access.

When answers to questions weren't so easy to find.
When answers to questions weren't in our hands.
When answers to questions was a journey in itself.

A time when we weren't all connected.
A time when gatherings were truly meant for stories.
A time when seeing each other in person had more meaning.

When we had to put in effort to see our friends.
Across the park.
Across the country.
Across the world.

A time when we weren't entitled.
A time when we weren't judged.
A time when we weren't in fear.

I do miss the simpler life.

A life you didn't need to follow.
A life you didn't need to like.
A life you didn't need to subscribe.

A life.
Where all you had to do.
Is connect.

Where less was demanded.
Where less was known.
Where less was available.

We could truly enjoy our lives.
We could truly live in the moment.
We could truly look forward to something.

With all of our emotion.
With all of our might.
With all of our power.

Just waiting for that moment to share more stories.
And be one with each other.
Without the other knowing all the details in between.

I do miss the simpler life.

Love.
- Yourself

Utter Those Words.

Dear Me.

It's okay.

It's okay to go back.

To when you fell in love.
To when you thought times were good.
To when you felt complete.

To when your heart broke.
To when your life fell apart.
To when your world turned upside down.

It's only natural.
It means you are human.
It means you've come far.

And that moment happened.
To make you feel this way.
You have a heart my dear friend.

You have a heart.

You aren't so black and white.
Like you thought you were.

Just keep looking up.

Up at the moon.
Up at the clouds.
Up at the stars.

And utter those words.

Those words that you wish you always told.
Those words that you wish you always felt.
Those words that you wish you always meant.

And remember them.

For one day.
You may.
You will.

Say it all over again.

Love.
- Yourself

Mud.

Dear Me.

It feels like mud.
Like pushing a block up a mountain.
Like a rope tying you down.

But if you want it that bad.
To reach pure freedom.

Then that's how hard you have to work.
You have to push harder.
You have to fight.

Beyond all the pain.

To call yourself whole.

You're close.
Don't stop now.

Keep going.

Love.
- Yourself

I've Been Patient.

Dear Me.

Can you let it go yet.

It's been quite some time now.

And I've been patient.

It's time.

It's time you moved on.

Onto bigger.
Better things.

The next stage.
The next chapter.

Immerse yourself into it.
Dive into it all.

It's waiting.
and so am I.

Let go.

Love.
- Yourself

Get Off It.

Dear Me.

I'm not trying to sound like a smart ass.
But you know how it's designed.
How it functions.
Because you have to know this shit.
For a living.
It's your career.

So get off it.

Don't you get it.
That device in your hand.

Yes. Your phone.

The software living inside it.
The applications living inside the software.
The businesses living inside the applications.

They are designing your experience.
Based on your interactions.
Your device has become an extension of you.

When you feel positive.
You interact with positive things.
Which makes it think you want more of it.
So it gives you more positive.
Forever.

Sadly.
The opposite is also true.
And it can send you into an endless spiral.
Of negativity. Of darkness.

Stay.
Stay in the light.

Use it for good.
Use it to create.
Create something beautiful.
Something elegant.
Something pristine.

Or get off it.

Everything else will follow.

Love.
-Yourself

What A Beautiful Thing.

Dear Love.

I can feel you fading.
As someone I knew.
I knew in the past.

It hurts.
But it's less painful.

I've been alone in this darkness.
For so long.

But I guess what they say is true.

"Time does heal."
"It gets better with time."

What a beautiful thing.
That the one thing we can't control.

Is the one thing that will heal.

Heal brokenness.
Heal darkness.
Heal a heart.

You refused it to be true.
In the moment.
You wanted it to last forever.

But you know what.
That's the journey.

We can't control time.
But we can control what we do with it.

I'm sorry.
and...
Thank you.

I Love.
- You.

I'm Sorry.

Dear Me.

I'm sorry.
I'm sorry that I couldn't save you.

I can't say it enough.

And it's a memory that I will live with.
For the rest of my life.

It hurts my soul knowing that I've failed.
I've failed to show you the light in the moment.
I've failed for so long.

Heaven knows I've tried.
I've tried for so long.

And because of my failure.
I have to leave you.

To let go and reset.
To leave it all behind and start anew.
Start a new chapter.

Because.
When I think about those dark days.

I want to know they happened for a reason.
I want to know that we've grown from it.
I want to know that I won't live those days in regret.

And that can only happen over time.

I can't apologize enough.
I can't thank you enough.

What is meant to be.
Is meant to be.
I'm sorry.

Love.
- Yourself

The Lost Souls.

Dear Me.

Fuckin' hell if you have to suffer for their mistakes.

Don't get dragged down.
Don't get pulled into their shit.

You can.
You will.
Be better than them.

The lost souls.
Fuck em'.

Don't waste your time.
Like they are.

Ignore the bullshit.
Embrace yourself.

Don't bring anyone into your mess.
Deal with it yourself.

Your problems are yours.
No one the fuck else's.

Deal with it.
Learn from it.

Apologize to yourself.
Forgive yourself.

Then move onto the next big thing.

With a tamed ego.
With controlled emotions.
With new life lessons learned.

As you start to see it all come together.
That life is the greatest teacher.

Love.
- Yourself

Grow The Fuck Up.

Dear Me.

How can one person fuck you over so much.
Because of their lack of responsibility.

You still care.
But you don't know if you should.

Your heart wants to keep it together.
Your brain wants to scream.

Let this be a hard life lesson.
To never forget your responsibilities.

To your family.
To your children.
To your close friends.
To the world.

Leave an impact with your work.
Lead by example.

I will say it once.
I will say it again.

*"With great power.
Comes great responsibility."*

Never forget this.
You have an obligation.
To this planet.

You have to think bigger than yourself.
Or you're going to not only fuck over yourself.
But you're going to fuck over those who you are closest to you.

By no clear intention of your own.
That's just how our society works.

And that.
Is the cold hard truth.

So get your shit together.
And own it.
Stay accountable.
Stay responsible.

And do not bring others into your fucking mess.

Grow the fuck up.

Love.
-Yourself

You Need More Time.

Dear Me.

I can't believe how deep your emotions run.
No matter how much you want to run from it.
It keeps pulling you back in.
Looming over you.
Haunting you.

The sadness.
The anger.
The happiness.

It all comes back.
You can't make sense of it.

And that is the most frustrating thing.
It doesn't make sense.
It makes no fucking sense.

I guess you really do need more time.
More time to fight it.

Your mind needs more help.
And the only thing that will support you now.
Is time.

You will find zen again.
I know it.
But it's not now.
But you will.

Trust me.

Love.
- Yourself

Where Hell Is.

Dear Me.

I'm the only one who cared.
I'm the only one who cared about your future.
I'm the only one who cared about your growth.

I didn't care about what happens in the now.
I didn't care about what happened yesterday.
Until it started affecting your future.

How much time you wasted.
How many incompetent friends you've made.
How you got sucked into a dark hole of shit.

We all know what dark holes do.
It sucks in everything.
Light. Emotions. You.

And it's a place of lost souls.

Where hell is.
Where no one cares.
Where souls go to die.

And it's near impossible to escape.
It feels like everything is out to trap you.
Out to get you.
Out to make your life a living hell.

It's okay to go back.
To a time.

When you saw light.
Saw growth.
Saw your future.
Saw freedom.

It's okay to go back.
Find your way back.
To when you cared about your future.
Then move forward from there.

One step back.
Two steps forward.

Your life isn't over yet.
There's still much to do.

Love.
-Yourself

Deeper Than Darkness.

Dear Me.

She said.
Tell her everything.
Let loose every deep. dark. secret.
Trust her.

And you did.
You opened up everything.
You opened up more than ever before.
You trusted her.
To keep it locked up between us.

But there is more.
Even you are afraid.
Afraid of telling yourself.

Because of how much it will destroy you.
From the inside out.

It's locked up.

Deeper than darkness.
Darker than the blackest night.

But maybe that's the key.

Will you go there.

You know I got your back.

Always.

Love.
- Yourself

Dear Me.

Dear Me.

Made in
Toronto, Ontario
Canada

Made in the USA
Middletown, DE
04 October 2020

21114867R00054